CHIHULY
AT THE SALK

Portland Press

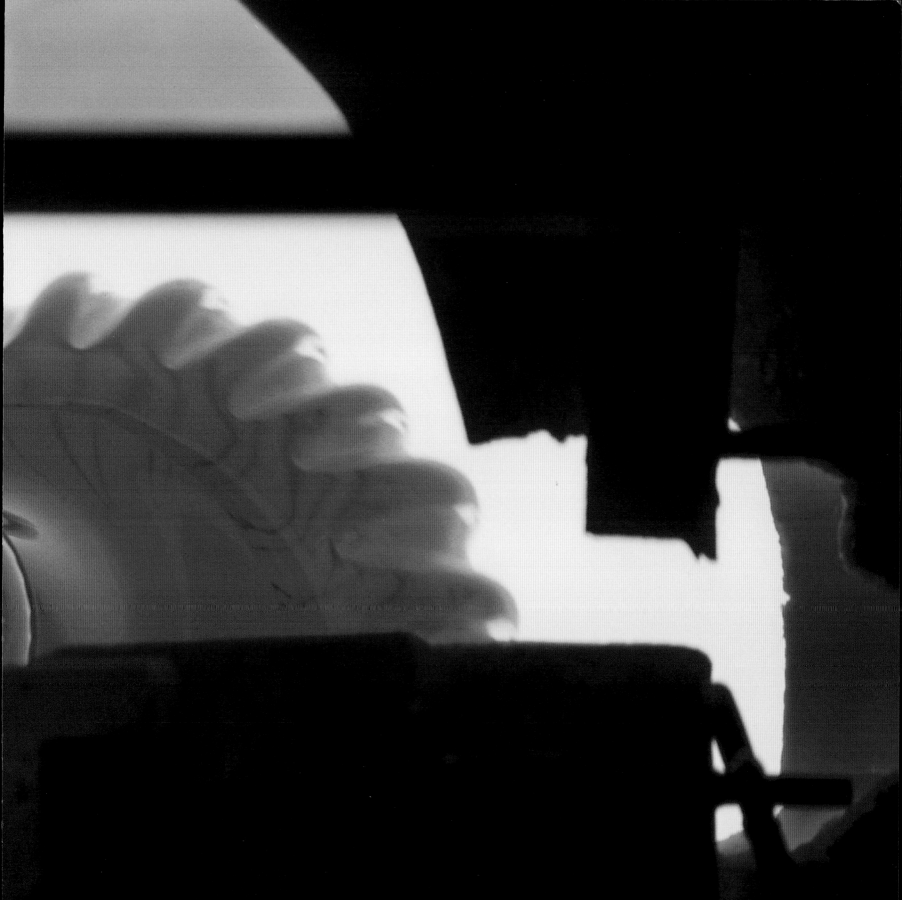

In celebration
of Jonas Salk
and Louis Kahn

Chihuly

What was your first exposure to architecture? I have always been interested in design and architecture. As a child of the 1950s, I was crazy about automobile design. I first noticed architecture as a young boy in Tacoma, Washington. I was fascinated with the warehouse district, the large beautiful wooden buildings, and Union Station. The Space Needle, which was built in 1962 for the World's Fair in Seattle, Washington, was another important icon. This compelled me to enroll in the University of Washington, where I received a B.A. in Interior Design in 1965.

How does light inform the architecture at the Salk? Well, you know I'm crazy about light. The manipulation of light is the most deliberate component of Louis Kahn's design for the Salk. In the fog or during an overcast day, the building reads as a beautiful, bleached monastic ruin sitting atop the Torrey Pines mesa. The daily trajectory of the sun, which ends up as a full-blown sunset at the end of the courtyard, is one of the most spectacular things I have ever seen. The monochromatic space comes alive as it's bathed by that California sunshine. I'm told the River of Life water feature is designed to line up perfectly with the sunset during the equinox.

What is special about Kahn's buildings at the Salk? The history of architecture, and to some extent the history of institution building, is about how well the client and the architect work together. It seems that Dr. Jonas Salk and Louis Kahn found the perfect balance.

How do you think the architecture embodies the scientific goals of Dr. Jonas Salk? My impression, and what I've been told by a number of the scientists who work there, is that the spaces are terrific to work in. The labs, which are built on an open plan without any supporting columns, are filled with light, even the floor below grade. The courtyard acts as a space to congregate and exchange ideas for persons from different disciplines and backgrounds, which in the process fosters creativity. It's hard to imagine how Louis Kahn could have made this function any better.

How did you select the installations to work with the architecture? Well, at first I was concerned when I learned there had never been a full exhibition of artwork in the courtyard. I knew the minute I considered working in that space that I had to put *The Sun* facing the Pacific Ocean and place *Black Niijima Floats* in and around the courtyard. The placement of the rest of the works is just my gut. I hope my artwork complements the site, as the Salk is truly a masterpiece on its own. The Salk was one of the most inspiring places to have ever staged my work.

– Dale Chihuly

The Boathouse, Seattle, Washington, 2010

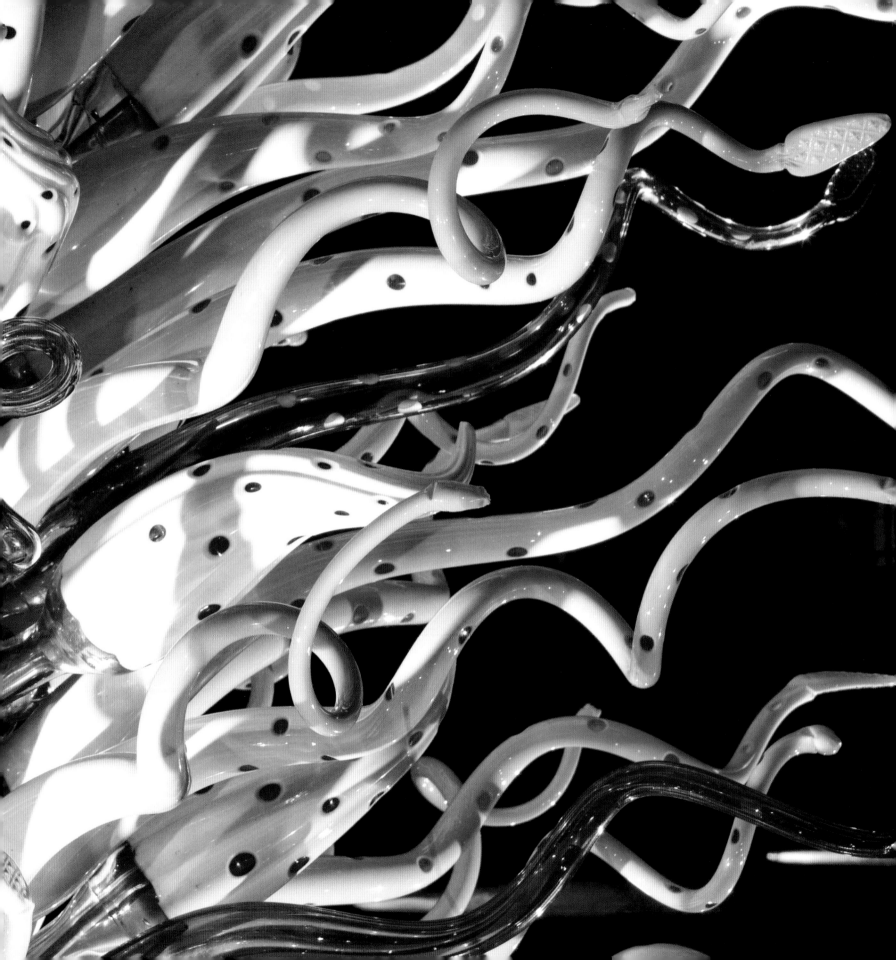

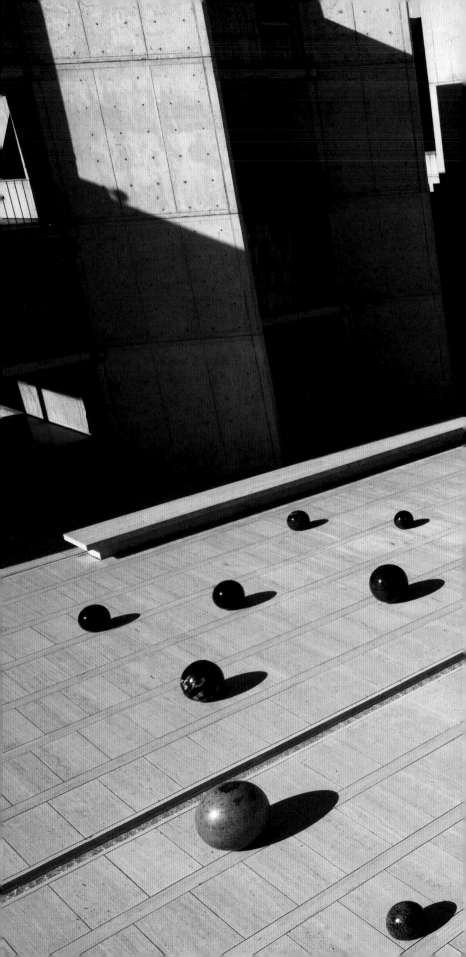

This book is dedicated to all the people
who made *Chihuly at the Salk* possible:

Joan and Irwin Jacobs

Dr. William Brody
Dr. Marsha Chandler

Rebecca Newman
Garry Van Gerpen
Kim Witmer

Tim Ball
Jennefer Collins
Jules De La Cruz
Allyson Collins Gobler
Julia Miller
Susan Trebach

Stacie Spector

Dr. William Alaynick

Faculty and Staff of the Salk Institute for Biological Studies

Team Chihuly

Image of Louis Kahn and Dr. Jonas Salk used with the kind permission
of their respective families.

 **SALK INSTITUTE**
FOR BIOLOGICAL STUDIES

Celebrating 50 years of scientific excellence in basic research. (1960-2010)

1941 Born September 20 in Tacoma, Washington, to George Chihuly and Viola Magnuson Chihuly.

1957 Older brother and only sibling, George, is killed in a Naval Air Force training accident in Pensacola, Florida.

1958 His father suffers a fatal heart attack at age 51. His mother goes to work to support Dale and herself.

1959 Graduates from high school in Tacoma. Enrolls in the College of Puget Sound (now the University of Puget Sound) in his hometown. Transfers to the University of Washington in Seattle to study interior design and architecture.

1961 Joins Delta Kappa Epsilon fraternity and becomes rush chairman. Learns to melt and fuse glass.

1962 Disillusioned with his studies, he leaves school and travels to Florence to study art. Discouraged by not being able to speak Italian, he leaves and travels to the Middle East.

1963 Works on a kibbutz in the Negev Desert. Returns to the University of Washington in the College of Arts and Sciences and studies under Hope Foote and Warren Hill. In a weaving class with Doris Brockway, he incorporates glass shards into woven tapestries.

1964 Returns to Europe, visits Leningrad, and makes the first of many trips to Ireland.

1965 Receives B.A. in Interior Design from the University of Washington. Experimenting on his own in his basement studio, Chihuly blows his first glass bubble by melting stained glass and using a metal pipe.

1966 Works as a commercial fisherman in Alaska to earn money for graduate school. Enters the University of Wisconsin at Madison, where he studies glassblowing under Harvey Littleton.

1967 Receives M.S. in Sculpture from the University of Wisconsin. Enrolls at the Rhode Island School of Design (RISD) in Providence, where he begins his exploration of environmental works using neon, argon, and blown glass. Awarded a Louis Comfort Tiffany Foundation Grant for work in glass. Italo Scanga, then on the faculty at Pennsylvania State University's Art Department, lectures at RISD, and the two begin a lifelong friendship.

1968 Receives M.F.A. in Ceramics from RISD. Awarded a Fulbright Fellowship, which enables him to travel and work in Europe. Becomes the first American glassblower to work in the Venini factory on the island of Murano. Returns to the United States and spends four consecutive summers teaching at Haystack Mountain School of Crafts in Deer Isle, Maine.

1969 Travels again throughout Europe and meets glass masters Erwin Eisch in Germany and Jaroslava Brychtová and Stanislav Libenský in Czechoslovakia. Returning to the United States, Chihuly establishes the glass program at RISD, where he teaches for the next fifteen years.

1970 Meets James Carpenter, a student in the RISD Illustration Department, and they begin a four-year collaboration.

1971 On the site of a tree farm owned by Seattle art patrons Anne Gould Hauberg and John Hauberg, the Pilchuck Glass School experiment is started. Chihuly's first environmental installation at Pilchuck is created that summer. He resumes teaching at RISD and creates *20,000 Pounds of Ice and Neon*, *Glass Forest #1*, and *Glass Forest #2* with James Carpenter, installations that prefigure later environmental works by Chihuly.

1972 Continues to collaborate with Carpenter on large-scale architectural projects. They create *Rondel Door and Cast Glass Door* at Pilchuck. Back in Providence, they create *Dry Ice, Bent Glass and Neon*, a conceptual breakthrough.

1974 Supported by a National Endowment for the Arts grant at Pilchuck, James Carpenter, a group of students, and he develop a technique for picking up glass thread drawings. In December at RISD, he completes his last collaborative project with Carpenter, *Corning Wall*.

1975 At RISD, begins series of *Navajo Blanket Cylinders*. Kate Elliott and, later, Flora C. Mace fabricate the complex thread drawings. He receives the first of two National Endowment for the Arts Individual Artist grants. Artist-in-residence with Seaver Leslie at Artpark, on the Niagara Gorge, in New York State. Begins *Irish Cylinders* and *Ulysses Cylinders* with Leslie and Mace.

1976 An automobile accident in England leaves him, after weeks in the hospital and 256 stitches in his face, without sight in his left eye and with permanent damage to his right ankle and foot. After recuperating, he returns to Providence to serve as head of the Department of Sculpture and the Program in Glass at RISD. Henry Geldzahler, curator of contemporary art at the Metropolitan Museum of Art in New York, acquires three *Navajo Blanket Cylinders* for the museum's collection. This is a turning point in Chihuly's career, and a friendship between artist and curator commences.

1977 Inspired by Northwest Coast Indian baskets he sees at the Washington State Historical Society in Tacoma, begins the *Basket* series at Pilchuck over the summer, with Benjamin Moore as his gaffer. Continues his bicoastal teaching assignments, dividing his time between Rhode Island and the Pacific Northwest.

1978 Meets William Morris, a student at Pilchuck Glass School, and the two begin a close, eight-year working relationship. A solo show curated by Michael W. Monroe at the Renwick Gallery, Smithsonian Institution, in Washington, D.C., is another career milestone.

1979 Dislocates his shoulder in a bodysurfing accident and relinquishes the gaffer position for good. William Morris becomes his chief gaffer for the next several years. Chihuly begins to make drawings as a way to communicate his designs.

1980 Resigns his teaching position at RISD. He returns there periodically during the 1980s as artist-in-residence. Begins *Seaform* series at Pilchuck in the summer and later, back in Providence, returns to architectural installations with the creation of windows for the Shaare Emeth Synagogue in St. Louis, Missouri.

1981 Begins *Macchia* series.

1982 First major catalog is published: *Chihuly Glass*, designed by RISD colleague and friend Malcolm Grear.

1983 Returns to the Pacific Northwest after sixteen years on the East Coast. Works at Pilchuck in the fall and winter, further developing the *Macchia* series with William Morris as chief gaffer.

1984 Begins work on the *Soft Cylinder* series, with Flora C. Mace and Joey Kirkpatrick executing the glass drawings.

1985 Begins working hot glass on a larger scale and creates several site-specific installations.

1986 Begins *Persian* series with Martin Blank as gaffer, assisted by Robbie Miller. With the opening of *Dale Chihuly objets de verre* at the Musée des Arts Décoratifs, Palais du Louvre, in Paris, he becomes one of only four American artists to have had a one-person exhibition at the Louvre.

1987 Establishes his first hotshop in the Van de Kamp Building near Lake Union, Seattle. Begins association with artist Parks Anderson. Marries playwright Sylvia Peto.

1988 Inspired by a private collection of Italian Art Deco glass, Chihuly begins *Venetian* series. Working from Chihuly's drawings, Lino Tagliapietra serves as gaffer.

1989 With Italian glass masters Lino Tagliapietra, Pino Signoretto, and a team of glassblowers at Pilchuck Glass School, begins *Putti* series. Working with Tagliapietra, Chihuly creates *Ikebana* series, inspired by his travels to Japan and exposure to ikebana masters.

1990 Purchases the historic Pocock Building located on Lake Union, realizing his dream of being on the water in Seattle. Renovates the building and names it The Boathouse, for use as a studio, hotshop, and archives. Travels to Japan.

1991 Begins *Niijima Float* series with Richard Royal as gaffer, creating some of the largest pieces of glass ever blown by hand. Completes a number of architectural installations. He and Sylvia Peto divorce.

1992 Begins *Chandelier* series with a hanging sculpture at the Seattle Art Museum. Designs sets for Seattle Opera production of Debussy's *Pelléas et Mélisande*.

1993 Begins *Piccolo Venetian* series with Lino Tagliapietra. Creates *100,000 Pounds of Ice and Neon*, a temporary installation in the Tacoma Dome, Tacoma, Washington.

1994 Creates five installations for Tacoma's Union Station Federal Courthouse. Hilltop Artists, a glassblowing program in Tacoma, Washington, for at-risk youths, is created by friend Kathy Kaperick and supported by Chihuly. Within two years, the program partners with Tacoma Public Schools.

1995 *Chihuly Over Venice* begins with a glassblowing session in Nuutajärvi, Finland, and a subsequent blow at the Waterford Crystal factory, Ireland.

1996 *Chihuly Over Venice* continues with a blow in Monterrey, Mexico, and culminates with the installation of fourteen *Chandeliers* at various sites in Venice. Creates his first permanent outdoor installation, *Icicle Creek Chandelier*.

1997 Continues and expands series of experimental plastics he calls "Polyvitro." *Chihuly* is designed by Massimo Vignelli and copublished by Harry N. Abrams, Inc., New York, and Portland Press, Seattle. A permanent installation of Chihuly's work opens at the Hakone Glass Forest, Ukai Museum, in Hakone, Japan.

1998 Chihuly is invited to Sydney, Australia, with his team to participate in the Sydney Arts Festival. A son, Jackson Viola Chihuly, is born February 12 to Dale Chihuly and Leslie Jackson. Creates architectural installations for Benaroya Hall, Seattle; Bellagio, Las Vegas; and Atlantis, the Bahamas.

1999 Begins *Jerusalem Cylinder* series with gaffer James Mongrain in concert with Flora C. Mace and Joey Kirkpatrick. Mounts his most challenging exhibition: *Chihuly in the Light of Jerusalem 2000*, at the Tower of David Museum of the History of Jerusalem. Outside the museum, he creates a sixty-foot wall from twenty-four massive blocks of ice shipped from Alaska.

2000 Creates *La Tour de Lumière* sculpture as part of the exhibition *Contemporary American Sculpture* in Monte Carlo. Marlborough Gallery represents Chihuly. More than a million visitors enter the Tower of David Museum to see *Chihuly in the Light of Jerusalem 2000*, breaking the world attendance record for a temporary exhibition during 1999–2000.

2001 *Chihuly at the V&A* opens at the Victoria and Albert Museum in London. Exhibits at Marlborough Gallery, New York and London. Groups a series of *Chandeliers* for the first time to create an installation for the Mayo Clinic in Rochester, Minnesota. Presents his first major glasshouse exhibition, *Chihuly in the Park: A Garden of Glass*, at the Garfield Park Conservatory, Chicago. Artist Italo Scanga dies; he was a friend and mentor for more than three decades.

2002 Creates installations for the Salt Lake 2002 Olympic Winter Games. The Chihuly Bridge of Glass, conceived by Chihuly and designed in collaboration with Arthur Andersson of Andersson•Wise Architects, is dedicated in Tacoma, Washington.

2003 Begins the *Fiori* series with gaffer Joey DeCamp for the opening exhibition at the Tacoma Art Museum's new building. TAM designs a permanent installation for its collection of his works. *Chihuly at the Conservatory* opens at the Franklin Park Conservatory, Columbus, Ohio.

2004 Creates new forms in his *Fiori* series for an exhibition at Marlborough Gallery, New York. The Orlando Museum of Art and the Museum of Fine Arts, St. Petersburg, Florida, become the first museums to collaborate and present simultaneous major exhibitions of his work. Presents a glasshouse exhibition at Atlanta Botanical Garden.

2005 Marries Leslie Jackson. Mounts a major garden exhibition at the Royal Botanic Gardens, Kew, outside London. Shows at Marlborough Monaco and Marlborough London. Exhibits at the Fairchild Tropical Botanic Garden, Coral Gables, Florida.

2006 Mother, Viola, dies at the age of ninety-eight in Tacoma, Washington. Begins *Black* series with a *Cylinder* blow. Presents glasshouse exhibitions at the Missouri Botanical Garden and the New York Botanical Garden. *Chihuly in Tacoma*—hotshop sessions at the Museum of Glass—reunites Chihuly and glassblowers from important periods in his artistic development. The film *Chihuly in the Hotshop* documents this event.

2007 Exhibits at the Phipps Conservatory and Botanical Gardens, Pittsburgh. Creates stage sets for the Seattle Symphony's production of Béla Bartók's opera *Bluebeard's Castle*.

2008 Presents his most ambitious exhibition to date at the de Young Museum, San Francisco. Returns to his alma mater with an exhibition at the RISD Museum of Art. Exhibits at the Desert Botanical Garden in Phoenix.

2009 Begins *Silvered* series. Mounts a garden exhibition at the Franklin Park Conservatory, Columbus, Ohio. Participates in the 53rd Venice Biennale with a *Mille Fiori* installation. Creates largest commission with multiple installations at the island resort of Sentosa, Singapore.

COLOPHON

This first printing of CHIHULY AT THE SALK is limited to 3,500 casebound copies.
© 2010 Portland Press. All rights reserved. DVD is for private home viewing only.

Photography
Joe Belcovson (courtesy Salk Institute), Marc Lieberman (courtesy Salk Institute),
Terry Rishel, Dave Rosencrans

Design
Janná Giles and Billy O'Neill

Typefaces
Goudy and Meta

Paper
157 gsm matte art

Printed and bound
In China by Global PSD

Portland Press
PO Box 70856, Seattle, Washington 98127
800 574 7272 · www.portlandpress.net

ISBN: 978-1-57684-186-0